GREECE
the culture
Sierra Adare

A Bobbie Kalman Book
The Lands, Peoples, and Cultures Series

 Crabtree Publishing Company

The Lands, Peoples, and Cultures Series

Created by Bobbie Kalman

Editors
Virginia Mainprize
Greg Nickles
Ellen Rodger

Computer technology advisor
Robert MacGregor

Project development, writing, and design
Water Buffalo Books
Mark Sachner
Sabine Beaupré
MaryLee Knowlton

Separations and film
Dot 'n Line Image Inc.

Printer
Worzalla Publishing Company

Illustrations
Susan Tolonen: page 15, back cover

Special thanks to
The Greek Tourism Office and Office of the Minister of Business, New York; Gonda Van Steen, Department of Classics, University of Arizona; the Panos family; Marsha Baddeley

Photographs
Susan Alworth: page 26; Arthus/Explorer/Photo Researchers: page 25 (bottom); Bachmann/Photo Researchers: page 20 (bottom left); Corbis-Bettmann: page 12 (bottom); Marc Crabtree: pages 19 (bottom), 23 (top left), 30; Robert Fried/Tom Stack & Associates: cover, pages 16–17, 20 (top left and right, bottom right); Richard Frieman/Photo Researchers: page 21; Ronny Jaques/Photo Researchers: page 23 (top right); Wolfgang Kaehler: pages 1, 3, 6 (bottom), 10, 11 (top), 24 (top), 27; Noboru Komine/Photo Researchers: page 31; Erich Lessing/Art Resource, NY: pages 6 (top), 8 (both), 17, 28–29; Will & Deni McIntrye/Photo Researchers: pages 4–5, Matsumoto/Explorer/Photo Researchers: page 24 (bottom); Hans Namuth/Photo Researchers: page 18 (top); Photo Researchers: page 11 (bottom); Carl Purcell: pages 14, 18 (bottom), 23 (bottom left); Scala/Art Resource, NY: pages 9 (both), 12 (top), 13; Thomas/Explorer/Photo Researchers: page 19 (top); Leonard von Matt/Photo Researchers: page 7; Wysocki/Explorer: Photo Researchers: page 25 (top).

Front cover: For festivals and special occasions, people in the province of Epirus, in western Greece, wear traditional costumes.

Title page: These dolphins, which are part of an almost 4000-year-old fresco in the palace of Knossos on the Greek island of Crete, seem to be leaping right out of the water.

Back cover: Olives and olive oil have been part of the Greek diet since ancient times. This vase, which was made in the sixth century BC, shows men harvesting ripe olives by beating an olive tree with long poles.

Published by
Crabtree Publishing Company

350 Fifth Avenue	360 York Road, RR 4	73 Lime Walk
Suite 3308	Niagara-on-the-Lake	Headington
New York	Ontario, Canada	Oxford OX3 7AD
N.Y. 10118	L0S 1J0	United Kingdom

Cataloging in Publication Data
Adare, Sierra.
    Greece: the culture / Sierra Adare.
        p. cm. -- (The lands, peoples, and cultures series)
    Includes index.
        Summary: Focuses on the ancient arts and modern treasures of Greece, introducing its mythology, crafts, foods, festivals, and Olympic games.
        ISBN 0-86505-308-1 (paper).-- ISBN 0-86505-228-X (RLB)
        1. Greece--Civilization--Juvenile literature. [1. Greece-Civilization.] I. Title. II Series: Kalman, Bobbie. 1947-Lands, peoples, and cultures series.
DF77. A33 1999
949.5--dc21   98-38944
                                                                 CIP

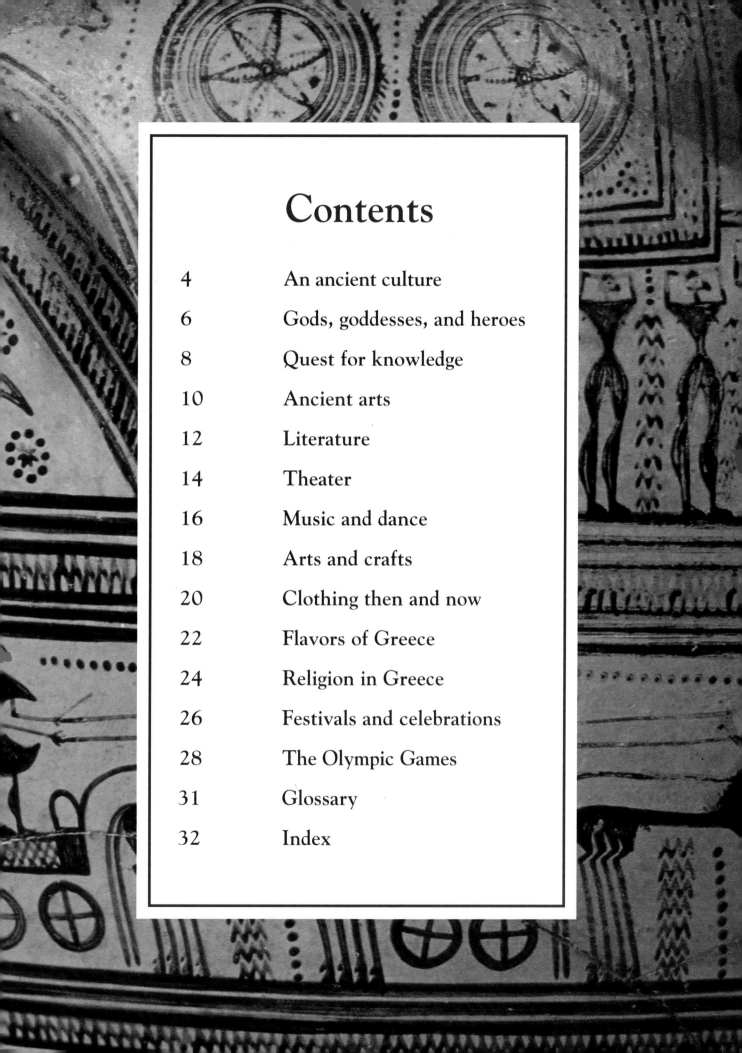

Contents

4   An ancient culture

6   Gods, goddesses, and heroes

8   Quest for knowledge

10   Ancient arts

12   Literature

14   Theater

16   Music and dance

18   Arts and crafts

20   Clothing then and now

22   Flavors of Greece

24   Religion in Greece

26   Festivals and celebrations

28   The Olympic Games

31   Glossary

32   Index

⚏ An ancient culture ⚏

Many of our ideas, beliefs, and outlooks, from the study of the stars to thoughts about what makes **architecture** and art beautiful, come from the ancient Greeks. Their ideas about medicine, mathematics, and **democracy**, about sport, **philosophy**, theater, and poetry have influenced our knowledge and attitudes today.

What is culture?

A people's culture is more than their art and beliefs. It includes the way people behave, the food they eat, and how their families live.

Greek culture: ancient and modern

Over the centuries, Greece has been invaded by other people, including the Macedonians, the Romans, and the Turks. Some of these invaders adopted Greece's unique culture and spread it around the ancient world. The Greeks, too, absorbed some of the culture of these people, much as sponges off the coast absorb salt from the sea.

Today's Greek culture combines the old and the new. Drawing strength from a rich past that goes

back five thousand years, modern Greece is a young nation and has only recently become a fully democratic country. As in the past, modern Greeks are influenced by the culture of other people. They also offer their own rich culture to the rest of the world.

A family stands within an ancient gate in Mycenae, the home of one of the earliest Greek civilizations.

Gods, goddesses, and heroes

(above) An illustration on an ancient Greek jar shows Athena emerging from the forehead of Zeus.

(below) Apollo, one of the most beloved ancient gods.

Myths are stories that people make up to explain things they do not understand. The ancient Greeks created myths to explain why the seasons changed, why it stormed, or why people got sick. They believed that gods and goddesses controlled events in nature and the lives of humans. When things went wrong, it was because the gods were angry.

Feet of clay

Like the gods of many religions, the gods of the ancient Greeks were **immortal**. Unlike most gods, who usually show a higher standard of behavior than humans, the gods and goddesses of the ancient Greeks were not perfect creatures. They behaved much like humans. They were angry, jealous, and cunning. They fell in and out of love, played tricks on each other, and fought fiercely among themselves. They often caused trouble for each other and for the humans they ruled.

Zeus, king of the gods

Zeus ruled Mount Olympus, the **sacred** home of the gods. He controlled the sky and the weather and threw thunderbolts when he was angry. He wrapped Mount Olympus in clouds so people could not see what the gods were doing. According to the ancient Greeks, this was why mist covered the mountain most of the time.

Athena, goddess of war and wisdom

Athena, the **patron** goddess of the ancient city-state of Athens, was Zeus's daughter. According to myth, Zeus swallowed his pregnant wife Metis because he was afraid she would bear a son mightier than himself. Athena then sprang in full armor from Zeus's head.

Apollo, god of light and prophecy

Apollo was the son of the god Zeus and twin brother of Artemis the huntress, goddess of wild animals and childbirth. As the god of **prophecy**,

Apollo became more **revered** than his father. Worshippers from Greece and beyond flocked to his temple at Delphi. They came to consult the oracle, a priestess who gave advice and told the future.

Demeter, goddess of agriculture

Throughout history, people have tried to explain why seasons change. This is the story the ancient Greeks told:

Hades, the god of death, lived in a dark palace under the earth, where he ruled the ghosts of the dead. He fell in love with Persephone, Demeter's daughter. With Zeus's permission, Hades took her to live in the world of the dead. Demeter, the goddess of the harvest, was heartbroken at the loss of her beloved child. She forbade the trees to bear fruit and the grasses to grow. Cattle died of starvation, and famine hit the land. Something had to be done. Zeus ordered Persephone to stay with Hades half the year, but allowed her to return to earth and visit her mother for six months. When Persephone was with Demeter, plants came to life and grew. When she returned to the underworld, fall and winter began.

Perseus and Medusa

Perseus's mother, Danae, was being forced into marriage by an evil king. The king promised Perseus that he would leave Danae alone if he brought him the head of Medusa. Medusa was a gorgon, a winged monster with huge teeth and snakes for hair. Anyone who looked at her was turned to stone. Determined to kill Medusa, Perseus set out on his quest. Because he was Zeus's son, the gods gave him a pair of winged sandals, a strong sword, and a polished silver shield. Wearing the sandals, Perseus flew to the gorgon's island. Looking at her reflection in his shield, he fought Medusa and cut off her head. When he returned to tell the evil king that he had killed Medusa, Perseus found that he was still pestering Danae to marry him. Perseus was so angry that he forced the king to look at the head of Medusa and turned him into stone.

A clay tablet showing Persephone and Hades sitting on their throne. They are holding offerings to Demeter, Persephone's mother, the goddess of the harvest.

Write your own myth

Now that you have read some Greek myths, try to write one of your own. What would you like to explain? It may be where dreams come from, or why the moon changes its shape each month. Perhaps you might write a myth about why trees lose their leaves in the fall, why the wind makes a noise, or why leopards have spots. Reading myths will show you how other people have explained these things and will give you ideas. Now use your imagination and make up your own myth.

Seldom in the history of the world has a country had as many great scientists and thinkers as ancient Greece. Without the help of modern instruments, Greek mathematicians and **astronomers** made incredible discoveries. **Philosophers** developed ways of thinking and came to conclusions about the meaning of life that still affect our ideas today.

Hippocrates, the doctor

Hippocrates, a Greek **physician** who lived sometime around 460 to 377 BC, studied why people became sick. Instead of relying on the magic of the gods to cure his patients, Hippocrates used herbs and other natural treatments. Unlike other healers of the period, he believed that the human body was a single living thing and not many parts working independently. When people got sick in those days, they asked one god to heal their feet, another to cure their headache, and another to stop their stomach pains. Hippocrates believed in treating the whole body. His *Corpus*, a collection of 53 books on many medical topics, is still studied by medical students. Doctors also take the Hippocratic oath. Based on the practices of Hippocrates, it is a promise to treat patients in a professional and caring way.

Archimedes, mathematical genius

Would you believe that climbing out of a bath led to one of the great scientific discoveries? It is a good thing Archimedes liked to be clean, because bathing led him to the principle of specific gravity. This is a law of nature that says that a body in water loses as much weight as the weight of the water it displaces. Archimedes was so excited by his discovery that he is said to have jumped out of his bath and run through the streets naked, shouting, *"Eureka,"* ("I have found it.") His discovery led him to invent the Archimedes screw, a hand-cranked pump that raises water from one level to the other.

(above) The Hippocratic oath, a pledge made by doctors who practice medicine today, is named for this Greek physician, Hippocrates.

(below) Archimedes, shown on the left, was a mathematician and an engineer.

Geometry and Pythagoras

Pythagoras was a Greek mathematician. He used mathematics to figure out that the world was round instead of flat. His ideas about geometry — the measurement of lines, shapes, and angles — are taught in schools today.

Aristarchus, scientist of the stars

A mathematician and astronomer who lived around 270 BC, Aristarchus was the first scientist to say that the earth spun on its own axis and that it revolved around the sun. Then and for centuries later, most people wanted to believe that the earth was the center of things. They refused to accept this incredible discovery. Without precise instruments, Aristarchus also figured out how long it took the earth to revolve around the sun. His estimate of the length of the year was only seven minutes and sixteen seconds too short!

Socrates, the questioner

In Greek, *philosopher* means "lover of wisdom." Socrates lived in the ancient city-state of Athens from 470-399 BC. He spent his life thinking about truth and the nature of good and evil. Socrates encouraged people to think for themselves. He thought they should question their superstitions about magic and their beliefs in the gods. Because he questioned the ideas that were popular at the time, Socrates seemed dangerous to the people in power. He was condemned to death. As was the custom, Socrates was given the chance to kill himself. His weeping jailer brought him a cup of poison. Socrates bravely took the cup, drank the poison, and died. Today, he is considered one of the greatest of the world's philosophers.

Aristotle's quest for knowledge

If Socrates was a questioner, Aristotle was a knowledge seeker. Everything fascinated him. He studied and wrote about many topics, including the human soul, animals and plants, **astronomy**, the weather, and politics. Aristotle opened a philosophy school called the *Lyceum*.

Socrates (above) and Aristotle (below) were two Greek philosophers who taught us much about how we think, learn, and create art.

Art and architecture were very important to the ancient Greeks. **Artisans** created beautifully decorated pottery and fine gold jewelry. Architects designed magnificent monuments, temples, and public buildings, which are still copied today. Sculptors carved graceful marble statues that seem almost human.

Pictures on pots

Throughout the ancient world, Greek pottery was highly prized. Potters' wheels turned out jugs, drinking cups, perfume bottles, and vases in many shapes and sizes. Many pieces were so well made that they have survived for centuries. Greek traders sold pottery to eager buyers in exchange for grain, timber, rich fabrics, and dyes.

Looking at Greek pottery tells us a lot about how the Greeks lived, worked, and played. It also tells us about Greek traditions and religion, because many of the decorations portray Greek heroes, scenes from ancient myths, and stories about the gods and goddesses.

Wall paintings

Ancient Greek artists did not use paint and canvas. They created frescoes, paintings on wet plaster walls, some of which survive to this day. At the remains of the Minoan palace of Knossos, on the island of Crete, **archeologists** have discovered wall paintings that are as colorful today as they were 4000 years ago.

Sculpture

In ancient Greece, statues of gods and goddesses, mythical heroes, and real people decorated temples and the homes of the wealthy. Statues were part of the architecture of all public buildings, and they stood in the agora, the city marketplace. With special tools for drilling, sawing, and sanding, sculptors could work with hard marble as if it were clay.

(above) A krater is a large, two-handled bowl in which water and wine were mixed in ancient Greece and Rome. This krater, on display in Athens, is nearly 3000 years old!

(opposite page, top) An ancient fresco from the island of Crete shows two acrobats performing with a bull.

(opposite page, bottom right) Many buildings all over the world use elements of Greek architecture, especially column styles from ancient temples.

Fun and games

One of the everyday activities shown on Greek pots may surprise you. Ancient designs show people playing board games. The boards no longer exist, but pictures on pots show that people played these games at home and in public places, where the boards were often built right into a building. Other pots show boys enjoying ball games, rolling hoops, and playing a game much like hockey — without the ice!

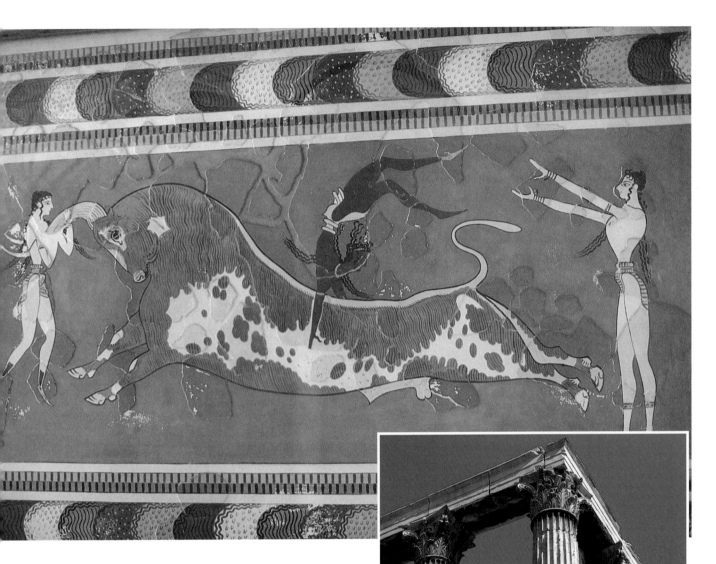

Architecture

Many buildings all over the world use elements of Greek architecture, especially column styles from ancient temples. The Greeks used three styles of beautifully carved columns to hold up the roofs of their buildings. The earliest column, the Doric, was simple and thick. It rose from the floor to a plain top, or capital. The Ionic column was thinner and more delicate. It had a carved scroll-like capital. From the fifth century BC, the Corinthian column became popular. It was topped with a capital decorated with carved scrolls and an acanthus design, featuring the leaves of the acanthus plant, which grows in countries around the Mediterranean Sea.

Thinner at the top

If you look at the columns of a Greek temple from a distance, they seem to rise up gracefully from the floor. Greek architects designed columns to **taper** slightly at the top. If they had been perfectly even, an **optical illusion** would make them look thinner in the middle.

Two scenes from Homer's epic poems, the **Iliad** and the **Odyssey**: (above) Penelope, the wife of the Greek hero Odysseus, sitting at her loom, waiting for her husband to return from war; (below) the Trojan horse, used by the Greeks to defeat the city of Troy.

Literature

Many types of writing that are common today have their beginnings with the ancient Greeks. These styles include long poems that tell a story, historical writing, accounts of travels to other parts of the world, and adventure stories.

Epic poetry

About 3000 years ago, Greece went through a period known as the Dark Ages. For centuries, the art of writing was lost, but people did not forget everything about their past. They preserved their history in epic poems, long stories with regular **rhythm**. These poems told of exciting adventures and brave deeds, and they were filled with colorful details. Epic poems were not written down but were memorized. They were often sung by traveling **minstrels** who added verses of their own to the songs of other poets.

The *Iliad* and the *Odyssey*

A poet named Homer composed what are probably the most famous epic poems of ancient Greece, the *Iliad* and the *Odyssey*. The stories are filled with battles and shipwrecks, duels with monsters, and touching love affairs. They also tell the story of the Trojan War between the Greeks and the people of the city of Troy. Greek soldiers attacked Troy but could not break down the city's walls. The long siege ended with a trick. The Greeks left a huge wooden horse outside the gates of Troy and pretended to sail away. Thinking the horse was a mysterious gift, the Trojans dragged it into the city. At night, Greek soldiers, hidden inside the horse, crept out. They opened the gates to their fellow warriors and captured Troy.

The *Odyssey* is the story of the travels and adventures of the Greek hero Odysseus (also known as Ulysses) in the ten years of his journey home after the Trojan War. In modern English, the word "odyssey" is used to describe a long and adventurous journey.

Herodotus, the travel writer

During the fifth century BC, Herodotus wrote long histories of the period in simple **prose**. He traveled around the Mediterranean and wrote down what he saw and heard. His volumes describe the land, customs, legends, wars, and lives of the people he met. Herodotus wrote down stories as they were told to him. He let his readers decide for themselves if the details were true. Would you believe a story about headless men who had eyes in their chests, or giant bats guarding Asian lakes, or sailors who claimed to have sailed around Africa? Some of Herodotus's readers did.

Keeping the epic tradition

During the 400 years Greece was ruled by the Turks, the Greeks kept their traditions and values alive in folk songs. These songs told the stories of "outlaws," Greek heroes who fought against the Turks. Like epic poems, these folk songs were memorized and passed down from **generation** to generation.

Modern literature

Poetry is extremely popular in Greece today, and modern Greek poets are considered among the best in the world. Poetry is not only studied in school and read in private, but it is a form of entertainment performed in public. Like rock stars in North America, Greek poets perform their work in soccer stadiums filled with fans. Two of Greece's best-known modern poets, George Seféris and Odysséus Elytis, write about the mythology and glory of ancient Greece. Both have won Nobel Prizes in Literature. Composer Míkis Theodorákis has set many of their poems to music. Novelist Nikos Kazantzákis, from the Greek island of Crete, is known throughout the world for his books *The Last Temptation of Christ* and *Zorba the Greek*. Both books have been translated into many languages and made into successful films.

The writings of Herodotus, known as the "father of history," are the earliest-known factual accounts of wars and other historical events.

Start your own oral tradition!

Show how a story changes by organizing a story circle of about five or six people. In private, tell a very short story to one person and have him or her tell it to another until everyone has heard the story. Then have the last person repeat the story. What has changed? Talk about why you think it has changed. Did people remember differently? Did people sometimes change the details to make the story better? Imagine this happening to stories told by many people over a long time. This is how oral tradition works.

🏛 Theater 🏛

Many of our ideas about modern **drama** come to us from the ancient Greeks. **Tragedy**, comedy, and **farce** were all performed in the theaters of the Greeks. In fact, the word "tragedy" comes from the ancient Greek word for a goat, the animal which was sacrificed on the first day of the drama festival held in Athens each year.

Theater for everyone

A visit to the theater was one of the most important events in a Greek town. Men, women, and children all attended plays in open-air, semi-circular amphitheaters. The audience sat in rows of stone seats built into a hillside. Theaters were so well built, even the people in the back rows could hear every word. As many as 18,000 people could attend a performance. Those who could not pay, got in free. Plays were put on once a month, and the performance lasted all day.

Tragedy and comedy

Three tragedies and one comedy were performed during a theater day. Greek tragedies told the stories of gods, goddesses, and heroes. They showed the foolishness of revenge and revealed the weaknesses of humans. They made the audience think about life and death, envy and hate, love and loyalty. The chorus, a group of singers and dancers in the background, helped the audience understand the deeper meaning of the play. They commented on the action, like a sportscaster does today. Men played all the parts, including those of women. People sitting far from the stage could not see the actor's face. To show which characters they were portraying, the actors wore large masks. So the audience would go home in a good mood, the day ended with a comedy, poking fun at life or maybe even the audience!

Ahead of their time

Sophocles, Aeschylus, and Euripides lived and wrote during the fifth century BC. They are considered the greatest writers of Greek tragedy. Although few of their plays have survived, those that exist are still performed in theaters all over the world. All three playwrights made great contributions to drama. For example, Aeschylus came up with the idea of putting more than one actor on stage at a time. Movable scenery, sound effects, and even lighting with mirrors were all used in Greek theaters.

through jokes and slapstick humor, and usually ends up in jail — until next time.

Modern shadow puppets

Shadow puppet theater, which came to Greece from Turkey, features several characters who appear from one episode to the next, much like characters on a television comedy or cartoon show. Karaghiózis, the main character in shadow puppet theater, is a poor, uneducated fellow, dressed in rags. In each episode he pretends to be a famous person. He always gives himself away

The puppets are cut from pieces of leather. White material, stretched across a frame, is the stage screen. The puppets are flat and are held against the back of the screen. A light behind them creates the shadows that the audience sees on the screen. The puppet master has many jobs. Besides operating the puppets, he must do voices in different accents and sometimes even plays an instrument — all at the same time!

(opposite page) The 2000-year-old theater at Epidaurus is still used by Greek theater groups.

(below) These puppets are held behind a piece of white material. Their shadows move across the screen.

🏛 Music and dance 🏛

Music and dance have been inseparable since the time of the ancient Greeks, and they are still important today. They express the sorrows and joys of everyday life.

Ancient Greek music and dance

The ancient Greeks believed that dance originated with the gods, and people performed dances at religious festivals. Residents of the warrior city-state of Sparta enjoyed military music, and their soldiers drilled to marches. Wealthy Greeks hired musicians and young female dancers to entertain them while they ate. Music was played to affect moods. Think of a party today and how the type of music affects how the guests feel.

Dancing into modern times

Today, dance and music are a part of family gatherings, weddings, and other celebrations. Traditional dances take two forms, shuffling and leaping. In shuffling dances, dancers step in time to the right or left to distinct rhythms and melodies, almost dragging their feet as they move. Shuffling is a more ancient dance that comes from the mountainous regions. A lot of strength goes into the fancy turns, jumps, and twisting moves of the leaping dances.

Before Christian soldiers, passing through the country on their way to war, brought couples dancing to Greece, people did not dance together. Even now, many dances are performed **solo**.

(above) *A fresco shows a* **cithara**, *a kind of lyre that was associated with Apollo, the god of music and poetry.*

(left) *A group of dancers in the mountainous region of Epirus wear traditional clothing as they perform at a local festival.*

Rembétika

Today, dance and music are a part of every festival and of weddings and funerals. *Rembétika* is a folk dance that is less than 100 years old. The dance is performed to music played on traditional instruments, such as the *bouzoúki*, a stringed instrument. Rembétika recalls the hardships and sorrows of life. It is considered the most original kind of music to come out of Greece in the last century.

Theodorákis, democratic composer

Drawing on musical traditions from both the east and the west, composer Míkis Theodorákis creates **ballads** about political and personal themes. In the 1960s, during Greece's military **dictatorship**, when the army controlled the government, Theodorákis was put in jail because his music was about democracy and freedom.

The army running the government did not allow Theodorákis's music to be played, and people caught listening to it were imprisoned and tortured.

The zygia

A *zygia* is an orchestra that plays traditional Greek music or European music with a Greek twist. On mainland Greece, the zygia consists of the violin, clarinet, lute, and *sandouri*, which is played by striking its steel strings with small hammers. In the province of Epirus, the orchestra also includes a drum, called a *daouli*, and a tambourine. On the island of Crete, the orchestra uses a stringed instrument called a lyre, instead of the violin.

▯ Arts and crafts ▯

The arts and crafts of Greece reflect the country's rich history and varied geographic terrain. Knitting and embroidery are time-honored traditions. More recently, tourism provides new markets for Greeks who work in the leather and pottery crafts.

From grandmother to granddaughter

Some of the best examples of Greek crafts come from the villages, where skills are handed down from generation to generation. Embroidered cloth, decorated with floral and geometric designs, is created by women who learn needlework from their mothers and grandmothers. They sell their embroidery in the local agora, or marketplace.

(top) Plates with traditional and ancient designs.

(left) Rugs and other crafts on display at a market.

Warm and cozy

Wool sweaters and rugs are made in regions where sheep and goats are raised. The thick, woven rugs are called *flokati*. They are soaked in water for three days to soften the wool. People from the town of Arachova hand weave brightly colored and patterned rugs, which are often used as bedspreads and wall hangings.

Something for everyone

City markets are filled with stalls selling fine brass and silver metalwork. Some vendors specialize in wood carvings and leather goods, such as purses, vests, and boots. Clay pottery, decorated with ancient designs, is a favorite among tourists looking for a souvenir. Greek jewelry, some of the most beautiful in the world, can be bought from sidewalk stalls or elegant jewelry shops.

(top) A village woman spins wool into yarn.

(right) Leather goods for sale at an Athens shop.

Clothing then and now

The ancient Greeks dressed in loose clothing. The basic garment for both men and women was a tunic, called a *chiton*, made from a rectangle of woven cloth. Women's chitons were ankle-length. Men's were usually shorter, to the knee, but long for special occasions. In cooler weather, men and women added a woolen cloak, or *himation*, that was draped around the body. Over the chiton, women might wear a *peplos*, a long, belted tube-shaped tunic, held together at the shoulders by two pins. Outside, both men and women wore leather sandals or shoes, if they could afford them.

Jewelry and perfume

Women wore finely crafted gold and silver bracelets, necklaces, and earrings for pierced ears. Jewelry was a sign of wealth and good fortune. According to legend, Hera, queen of the gods, captured Zeus's heart with her perfume and elegant earrings.

Nineteenth century fashion

After Greek independence from the Turks in 1830, the new Queen of Greece, Amalia, designed a national costume for women. Called the Amalia dress, it is a colored, ankle-length skirt, a gold, embroidered, velvet jacket worn over a white blouse, and a red cap with a long silk tassel.

(opposite page) Modern Greeks wear traditional folk costumes for festivals and celebrations (upper left and upper right).

(opposite page) This guard (lower left) and young boy at a festival (lower right) wear ceremonial clothing based on the traditional fustanella and red fez that Greek men wore in the late 1800s.

(right) Many widows in Greece wear black after the death of their husband.

By the 1880s, the men's national dress was a white *fustanella*, a knee-length pleated skirt, similar to a kilt, with four hundred tiny pleats which are said to represent the number of years the Turks ruled Greece. *Erzones*, the soldiers who guard the tomb of the unknown soldier in Athens, still wear the traditional fustanella costume — a skirt, a full-sleeved white shirt, embroidered vest, white stockings, red shoes with enormous pompoms, and a red cap with a tassel, called a fez.

Modern dress

Today, traditional Greek costumes are best seen in a museum. Most people dress like Americans and other Europeans. In areas where there are few tourists, clothes are more conservative. Women usually wear dresses, and men wear long pants. In very **remote** villages, women may still dress in **pantaloons**, tunics, and boots. A woolen scarf, trimmed with sequins and tassels, covers their hair.

⚱ Flavors of Greece ⚱

Food in Greece feeds more than just the body. It nourishes the soul. Women put great effort into preparing delicious dishes for the family. Meals are a social occasion, a time for conversation and stories, for laughter and fun, for getting together with family and relaxing with friends.

Ancient foods

The ancient Greeks stored oil, wine, and grain in large jars in the coolest rooms in the house. Breakfast was a simple meal of bread and wine. Meat was expensive and was served only on festival days. Everyday meals consisted of cheese, bread, olives, and vegetables in season. The sea provided plenty of fresh fish. Meals were cooked over a wood fire in the kitchen and were served on pottery or metal plates. Spoons and knives were the only utensils. Ancient Greeks, like the people of many cultures today, ate with their fingers.

Today's meals

Greeks are not big breakfast eaters. They enjoy a tiny cup of strong coffee and perhaps a piece of bread. A mid-morning snack of bread and cheese will tide them over until a late lunch. Dinner, the main meal, is eaten late, around 10 p.m., and lasts well into the night. It usually begins with tasty starters, such as marinated eggplant, fried octopus, or vine leaves stuffed with meat and rice. The main course may be fish or meat with vegetables and a salad. A special holiday treat is a whole lamb roasted on an open fire.

Never on a Sunday

Sunday lunch is an important family meal. Because families go to church in the morning, many women do not have time to cook lunch. They prepare the food on Saturday evening and take it to the local bakery in their own pots. On Sunday morning, the baker cooks the food in the bread oven, and by the time church is over, lunch is ready to take home.

Olives and olive oil

According to legend, Athena became patron goddess of Athens because she gave people the olive tree. At one time, the olive tree was so beloved that anyone who cut one down could be killed. Today, the olive tree is the symbol of peace and prosperity. For centuries, farmers have been growing olives for eating, and pressing them to make olive oil. Olive oil is still a staple in Greek cooking. It is used instead of butter for frying, and its robust flavor gives a unique taste to cooked foods and salads.

Yogurt: an addition to any meal

Thick, creamy yogurt is a part of almost every meal in Greece. A plate of *tsatzíki*, a dip made of yogurt, cucumber, and garlic, is often served at the beginning of a meal. A bowl of yogurt, sweetened with honey and sprinkled with walnuts, is a favorite dessert.

Sweet tooth?

This candy is quick to make and delicious, too. Ask someone who can use the stove to help you.

Amigthalo praline
1 1/4 cups sliced almonds
3 tablespoons butter or margarine
1/4 cup sugar
1 sheet of foil

Rub 2 tablespoons of butter onto the sheet of foil. Mix the almonds, 1 tablespoon of butter, and the sugar in a large skillet. Heat the almond mixture over medium-high heat, stirring constantly. When the almonds turn golden brown, remove them from the heat. Spread the almond mixture evenly over the buttered sheet of foil. Let it cool undisturbed. Break the candy into small pieces. This candy is also used as a crunchy topping for ice cream in Greece.

(above) Olives, olives, and more olives! They come in a variety of sizes, tastes, and even colors.

(top left) You don't have to be Greek to love gyros — a delicious combination of lamb and beef grilled on a spit.

(bottom left) This small, family-run shop in Athens serves a variety of food, such as pastries, drinks, and gyros.

Religion in Greece

The ancient Greeks believed in and worshiped many gods and goddesses. Today, the large majority of Greeks belong to the Eastern (or Greek) Orthodox Christian Church.

Ancient religion

The Greeks believed in hundreds of gods. There was a god of the sea and storms, of the arts, of wine, of fire, of war. There were goddesses of love and wisdom, the hunt, of marriage, childbirth, and the family. Every town, stream, and forest had its own god.

The rise of Christianity

Christianity came to Greece after the country became part of the Roman Empire. Roman emperors made Christianity the official religion. In 330 AD, the emperor Constantine moved the capital of the empire to the Greek city which was later known as Byzantium and is now called Istanbul. Today, Istanbul is the capital of Turkey. The Eastern Orthodox Church of Christ, as Greece's religion is officially called, developed independently from the church in Rome, which is known as the Roman Catholic Church.

Turkish occupation

When the Turks invaded Greece, they brought their religion, Islam, with them. Many Orthodox churches were turned into **mosques** during the 400 years of Turkish occupation. Although the Turks were more tolerant of other religions than many Christian countries at the time, this was a difficult time for Greek religion and culture. Priests and monks held secret classes for young people to keep Greek traditions alive.

The church today

Today, about 97 percent of Greeks follow the Greek Orthodox religion. Especially in the countryside and on the islands, the church is an important part of everyone's life. In some villages, there are almost as many churches, small chapels, and shrines, as there are houses. Church services are long, filled with music, and rich in tradition. Sunday mass is the most important service of the week and can last three hours. In church, women usually stand on the left and men on the right. Children are grouped together near the front. The lighting of candles and the kissing of **icons** are a part of every service. The priest, dressed in a long, black robe and round, high hat, is separated from the people by a beautifully decorated screen.

(above) Unlike Roman Catholic priests, Greek Orthodox priests can marry and have a family.

(opposite page, top and bottom; this page, top) Three views of the domes and bell towers of Orthodox churches.

25

Dressed in both traditional and modern clothing, these children parade through a street on the island of Hydra during a local celebration.

Festivals and celebrations

Like their ancient Greek ancestors, modern Greeks love a celebration. They are very **patriotic**, and national holidays, commemorating important historical events, are celebrated throughout the country. Religious festivals are strictly observed, following the traditions of many centuries.

Sacrifices to the gods

The ancient Greeks had so many religious festivals that celebrating them all took up two months of the year. Festivals were a time of feasting, processions, song and dance, and sports competitions. They were more than a chance to have a good time, however. Festivals were based on the idea that sacrifices must be offered to please the many gods and goddesses of ancient Greece.

Religious festivals began with a procession to the temple and the placing of gifts of gold and silver on a table in front of the god's statue. Then animals and food were sacrificed to the god at a huge outdoor altar in front of the temple. People decorated the animal, usually a bull, with **garlands** of ribbons and flowers. After the animal was killed and offered to the god, people feasted on the meat.

The Great Panathenaea

Every four years, the people of ancient Athens honored their patron goddess, Athena, with a huge festival known as the Great Panathenaea. Worshippers gathered in the agora and climbed up a road to the Parthenon, the temple dedicated to Athena. The procession was led by women wearing embroidered robes. Close behind, men herded the 100 cattle that would be sacrificed to the goddess. Rich men rode in horse-drawn chariots, women carried jugs of wine and trays of food on their heads, and excited children followed behind. After the cattle were killed and cooked, everyone shared in the feast.

The Parthenon was the site of the great festival honoring Athena.

Modern festivals and celebrations

Today, religious celebrations are still very important to the Greeks. The spring feast of Easter is the most important. The weeks before Lent, a period of fasting before Easter, are a time for carnivals and fun. Shrove Monday, two days before the first day of Lent, is a national holiday and a day for picnics and kite flying. Then for 40 days, Greeks prepare themselves for Easter. Many do not eat meat, and they do not party. All of Greece observes Good Friday, the day commemorating the death of Jesus, with fasting and solemn candle-light processions in the streets. At midnight the next day, Lent is over, and the joyous celebration of Easter begins. The churches are filled, the bells ring, firecrackers explode, and the Greeks celebrate all night with food and wine.

The Greek calender is filled with other religious and national holidays. On October 28, Greeks celebrate *Ohi*, or "no" day. It honors their country's refusal to allow Italian soldiers into Greece during World War II and Greece's resistance against Nazi Germany.

▌ The Olympic ▌ Games

The most important athletic event in the ancient Greek world was the Olympic Games. People traveled from all over Greece and its colonies to compete in or watch the events. Today's Olympics, which are a revival of the ancient games, also attract athletes and spectators from around the world.

The ancient Olympic Games

To honor the god Zeus, the ancient Greeks held a week-long sports festival every four years. Heralds traveled through the country announcing the games and declaring that all wars would stop during the event. The games were held on the plain at Olympia, a religious center devoted to the worship of Zeus. Events included foot races, **discus** and **javelin** throwing, long jumps, wrestling and boxing, and chariot races. There were no teams, and individual winners were crowned with a simple wreath of olive leaves. When they returned home, they were given a hero's welcome.

The Olympic Games were held for 617 years, from the first games in 776 BC until 393 AD, when the Christian emperor forbade festivals honoring the ancient gods and goddesses. The statue of Zeus was removed from Olympia and taken to Constantinople, the new capital of the empire. Olympia was abandoned, and neglect and earthquakes left the site in ruins.

Revival of the Games

Today's modern Olympics were started in 1896 by a French baron, Pierre de Coubertin. Impressed by students' participating in sports,

(Left) Three runners seem to float across an ancient vase.

de Coubertin decided to revive the ancient games. He sent letters to every country. In these letters, he pointed out the educational value of sports. Many countries agreed to participate in an Olympic event. It was only right that Athens, the capital city of modern Greece, should host the games. They were held in a marble stadium built in 143 AD and completely reconstructed for the 1896 Olympics.

Greece and the modern games

The Olympic Games have been held regularly since 1896. A long-distance run, the marathon, is a new event based on the triumph of the ancient Athenians over the Persians at Marathon, a plain close to Athens. After the victory, a runner was sent to Athens to announce the news. After running the entire distance, 26 miles (41.3 kilometers) non-stop, he delivered his message, *"Enikesame!"* ("We won"), collapsed, and died on the spot.

At every Olympics, wherever they are held, Greek athletes lead the parade at the opening ceremony. The Olympic torch is lit from the

The Athens Olympics: 2004
In 2004, Athens will host the Olympic Games. The city is busy preparing for the Games. Highways are being expanded, the subway system is being extended, a new airport is being built, stadiums are being constructed and new hotels are opening. The country is getting ready to look after the hundreds of thousands of tourists who will descend on Greece for the event.

ancient site of Olympia. Runners from around the world pass the flame to each other. If the distances are great or the flame has to cross the ocean, the torch, accompanied by its runners, is transported by train or airplane. The Olympic Games officially begin when the torch lights the flame in the host city during the dramatic opening ceremonies.

Remains of the temple of Zeus at Olympia. People gathered every four years at Olympia to hold athletic contests in Zeus's honor.

𝕀 Glossary 𝕀

acoustics The total effect of sound

archeologist A person who studies ancient remains

architecture The art of designing buildings

artisan A skilled manual worker

astronomer A person who studies the stars and planets

astronomy The science of studying the stars and planets.

ballad A story that is usually sung

democracy A system of government in which people elect their representatives

dictatorship A government in which one person has absolute power

discus A disk, usually made of rubber or wood, that is thrown for distance in a contest

drama A play

farce A ridiculous comedy

garland A wreath or rope of leaves or flowers

generation A single stage of a family

icon A religious picture, painted on wood, of a holy Christian person

immortal Living forever

javelin A light spear

minstrel A wandering singer, musician, or poet

mosque A building where Muslims worship

optical illusion Something that appears different from how it really looks

pantaloons Loose-fitting, full-cut trousers

patriotic Loving one's country

patron Someone who protects or supports someone or something

philosopher A person who studies the meaning of life

philosophy The study of the meaning of life

physician A doctor

prophecy A prediction, usually about the future

prose Any piece of writing that is not poetry

remote Faraway, distant

revere To respect deeply, to honor

rhythm A regular pattern of sounds

sacred Holy, religious

solo On one's own

taper To become narrower at one end

tragedy A story or play with a sad ending

Nearly 4000 years ago, the Minoan civilization flourished on the island of Crete. At the palace of Knossos, the king and his court lived in great luxury.

⬛ Index ⬛

Aeschylus 15
agora 10, 18, 27
Amalia dress 21
Amalia, queen 21
ancient Greeks 4, 6, 7, 10, 12, 14,16, 21, 22, 24, 2729
Apollo 6, 7, 17
Archimedes 8
architecture 4, 10-11
Aristarchus 9
Aristotle 9
art 4, 9, 10-11
arts and crafts 18-19
astronomy 8, 9
Athena 6, 22, 27,
Athens 6, 9, 14, 19, 21, 22-23, 27, 30
Byzantium 24
chorus 14
Christianity 24
church 22, 25
clothing 21
column, Corinthian 10
column, Doric 10
column, Ionic 10
comedy 14
Constantine 24
Constantinople 29
Corinthian column 10
Crete 10, 13, 17, 31
culture 4, 5, 25
dance 16-17, 27
de Coubertin, Pierre 29
Delphi 7
Demeter 7
democracy 4, 17
Doric column 10
drama 14
Easter 27
Eastern Orthodox Christian Church 24, 25

Elytis, Odysséus 13
embroidery 18
epic poetry 12,13
Epidaurus 15
Euripedes 15
farce 14
festival 27
fez 21
folk song 13
food 22-23
food, ancient 22
fresco 10, 17
fustanella 21
games 10, 29-30
geometry 9
god 9, 10, 14, 16, 27, 29
goddess 6, 10, 14, 27, 24, 29
Good Friday 27
Great Panathenaea 27
Hades 7
hero 10, 14
Herodutus 13
Hippocrates 8
Hippocratic oath 8
holidays 27
Homer 12
icon 25
Iliad 12
Ionic column 10
Islam 25`
Istanbul 24
jewelry 10, 19, 21
Kazantzákis, Nikos 13
Knossos, palace of 31
Lent 27
literature 12-13
Marathon 30
marathon race 30
mathematics 4, 8, 9
meals 22
medicine 4, 8

Mediterranean Sea 10, 13
Medusa 7
minstrel 12
mosque 25
Mount Olympus 6
music 16-17, 25
musical instrument 17
myth 6-7, 10
Nobel Prize in Literature 13
Odysseus 12
Odyssey 12
olive 22, 23, 29
olive oil 22
Olympia 29-30
Olympic Games 29-30
Parthenon 27
Persephone 7
philosopher 8, 9
philosophy 4, 9
poetry 4, 12, 13
pottery 10, 18, 19
Pythagoras 9
religion 6, 7, 10, 24-25
Romans 4, 8, 10, 24
rug 18, 19
sculpture 10
Seféris, George 13
shadow puppets 15
Sophocles 15
Sparta 16
sport 4, 27
temple 10, 27
theater 4, 14-15
Theodorákis, Míkis 13, 17
tourism 18, 19, 21
tragedy 14, 15
Trojan War 12
Turkey 15, 24
Turks 4, 13, 21, 25
yogurt 22
Zeus 6, 21, 29, 30

1 2 3 4 5 6 7 8 9 0 Printed in the USA 5 4 3 2 1 0 9 8